# The Journey Art of Fudge Making

## Delicious Fudge Recipes for All Your Baking Needs

# Contents

# Introduction

There are many different desserts that you can choose to make. Many families like to make cookies all throughout the year, cakes for those special birthdays, or even different parfaits and salads when they need to bring something to a potluck. But in some cases, you may want to go with a simple dessert that is easy to make, even though it looks a little complicated.

In this guidebook, we are going to take a look at some of the delicious fudge recipes you can make from home.

While you may have thought creating fudge was almost impossible and super time-consuming, all of the recipes in this guidebook are simple to use and allow you to have the good taste, without all the hassle.

Whether you are looking for a fudge recipe with lots of rich chocolate in it or you would like to go with one that has a hint of fruit or even peppermint, this guidebook has you covered. Let's dive right in and see some of the best fudge recipes for your needs!

# Oreo Fudge

Oreo and chocolate mix together to make some tasty fudge that you can bring along to any occasion.

**Prep Time**: 15 minutes

**Servings**: 20

**Cook Time**: 60 minutes

**Ingredients:**

- 1 c. crushed chocolate sandwich cookies

- 1/2 c. crumbled chocolate sandwich cookies
- 1 tsp. vanilla
- 1 jar marshmallow crème
- 2 c. white chocolate chips
- 2/3 c. evaporated milk
- 3/4 c. butter
- 3 c. white sugar

**Directions:**

1. Add some parchment paper to a baking pan. Add the milk, butter, and sugar to a pan and heat up for five minutes. Take off the heat and add the marshmallow crème and white chocolate chips into this and let melt.
2. Add the vanilla. Gently fold the half cup of crumbled cookies in and then pour into the pan. Sprinkle the 1 cup of cookies on top.
3. Allow to cool at room temperature before serving.

# Orange Chocolate Fudge

A bit of chocolate and a bit of orange combine to make this tasty treat. Keep it in the freezer for a way to cool down at the end of the day.

**Prep Time**: 10 minutes

**Servings**: 20

**Cook Time**: 2 hours

## Ingredients:

- 2 tsp. grated orange peel
- 1/2 c. pecans, chopped
- 1 can condensed milk
- 21/2 c. chocolate chips

## Directions:

1. Prepare a pan with some parchment paper. Melt the chocolate chips and condensed milk in a double broiler in the microwave. Stir to make smooth.
2. Take off the heat and add the orange peel and pecans. Pour into a prepared pan and chill for 2 hours before serving.

# Peanut Butter Fudge

Peanut butter and fudge mix together to make your very own Reese's any day of the week, for a fraction of the cost.

**Prep Time**: 15 minutes

**Servings**: 20

**Cook Time**: 60 minutes

**Ingredients:**

- 1 jar marshmallow crème

- 1 c. crunchy peanut butter
- 1 c. butter
- 1 can evaporated milk
- 4 c. sugar

**Directions:**

1. Prepare a baking dish with butter. Butter a saucepan. Add to the heat and combine 1 c. of butter with the milk and sugar. Heat up a bit.
2. Take off the heat and stir in the marshmallow crème and peanut butter in here, beating to make it smooth.
3. Pour into the baking dish and allow time to cool before slicing into squares.

# Orange Cream Fudge

It is so light and fluffy that you won't be able to believe how good it is for any occasion.

**Prep Time**: 15 minutes

**Servings**: 2-

**Cook Time**: 2 hours

**Ingredients:**

- 9 drops red food coloring

- 12 drops yellow food coloring
- 3 tsp. orange extract
- 1 pkg. white chocolate chips
- Jar marshmallow crème
- 3/4 c. butter
- 2/3 c. heavy cream
- 3 c. white sugar

**Directions:**

1. Prepare a pan and then take out a pan and heat up the butter, cream, and sugar. Heat to a soft ball stage.
2. Take off the heat and stir in the chocolate chips and marshmallow crème until melted. Reserve a cup and set aside.
3. Add the food coloring and orange flavor into this and pour into the pan. Add the crème mixture on top and then swirl around for decorative effect.
4. Chill for 2 hours and then serve.

# Maple Walnut Fudge

Maple and walnut will come together to provide some of the best tastes and flavors that you need.

**Prep Time**: 15 minutes

**Servings**: 20

**Cook Time**:60 minutes

**Ingredients:**

- 1/2 c. broken walnuts

- 1 tsp. maple flavored extract
- 1/4 c. butter
- 1 can sweet condensed milk
- 3 c. white chocolate chips

**Directions:**

1. Prepare a baking dish with some parchment paper, letting the ends hang over. Melt the butter, condensed milk, and white chocolate in a bowl in the microwave until melted.

2. Stir in the maple extract before adding the walnuts. Pour into a baking dish and let set for one hour. Lift the fudge out and cut into squares to serve.

# Peanut Chocolate Scotch Fudge

This one has so many flavors in it, you won't know how to get started. With a few ingredients, you will have the fudge of your dreams.

**Prep Time**: 15 minutes

**Servings**: 20

**Cook Time**: 60 minutes

## Ingredients:

- 1 jar marshmallow crème
- 1 tsp. vanilla
- 1 c. butterscotch chips
- 1 c. chocolate chips
- 3/4 c. peanut butter
- 3/4 c. milk
- 3 c. white sugar
- 3/4 c. butter

## Directions:

1. Prepare a baking dish. Take out a pan and melt the milk, sugar, and butter. Bring to a boil and stir constantly.
2. When melted, remove from the heat and add the butterscotch chips, chocolate chips, and peanut butter to melt.
3. Stir in the vanilla and marshmallow crème. Pour into the pan and chill until firm.

# Raspberry Truffle Fudge

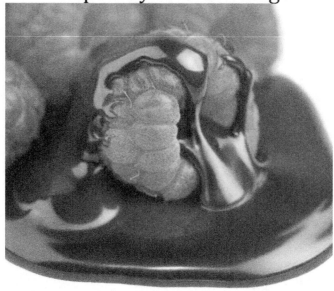

Raspberry and chocolate mix together to give you the flavors you need in this one. It is going to become one of your favorites in no time.

**Prep Time**: 5 minutes

**Servings**: 15

**Cook Time**: 60 minutes

## Ingredients:

- 2 c. chocolate chips
- 1/4 c. raspberry flavored liqueur
- 1/4 c. heavy cream
- Salt
- 1 1/2 tsp. vanilla
- 1 can sweetened condensed milk
- 3 c. chocolate chips

## Directions:

1. Prepare a baking pan with cooking spray and line with the wax paper. Combine the condensed milk and 3 cups chocolate chips in a microwave-safe bowl and heat up to melt the chocolate.
2. Add the vanilla and salt and spread everything into a pan to cool down. In a bowl, combine the cream with the liqueur and the rest of the chocolate chips.
3. Melt in the microwave and then pour over the fudge layer. Let it set for an hour before serving.

# Irish Cream Truffle Fudge

Irish cream isn't only good in your coffee. This is a great fudge to make for those long road trips or any other situation where you need something tasty to enjoy.

**Prep Time**: 15 minutes

**Servings**: 20

**Cook Time**: 60 minutes

## Ingredients:

- 2 Tbsp. butter
- 4 Tbsp. Irish cream liqueur
- 1/2 c. white chocolate chips
- 1 c. chocolate chips
- 1 1/2 c. nuts, chopped
- 1 c. Irish cream liqueur
- 3 c. confectioners' sugar
- 1/4 c. butter
- 3 c. chocolate chips

## Directions:

1. Prepare a baking pan with some butter. Set up a double boiler and melt 3 cups of chocolate chips with the 1 cup of white chocolate chips and 1/4 c. butter to make soft. Add in the Irish cream and confectioners' sugar. Place into the prepared pan and add some plastic wrap on top.

2. Make another double boiler and mix the rest of the chocolate to make soft. Take off the heat and add in the rest of the cream and butter to smooth.

3. Pour this over the cooled fudge and let set for an hour before serving.

# Cranberry Fudge

Cranberry can be a strong flavor to add into any dessert, but it tastes awesome as a fudge. Make a batch for later so you will have some to enjoy.

**Prep Time**: 15 minutes

**Servings**: 16

**Cook Time**: 60 minutes

## Ingredients:

- 1 tsp. vanilla
- 1/4 c. evaporated milk
- 1/2 c. confectioners' sugar
- 2 c. chocolate chips
- 1/2 c. corn syrup
- 1 pkg. cranberries

## Directions:

1. Prepare a pan with some plastic wrap. Heat up a pan and add the corn syrup and cranberries. Bring to a boil for 5 minutes before taking off the heat.
2. Add the chocolate chips, stirring to melt. Add the rest of the ingredients in and mix before pouring into a baking pan.
3. Cover and allow to chill for an hour before serving.

# Crispy Tiger Fudge

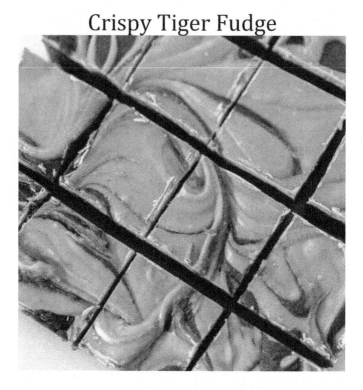

The appearance of this one can be a lot of fun, making it one of the options that you can make with the kids or when you really want to impress others.

**Prep Time**: 15 minutes

**Servings**: 4

**Cook Time**: 10 minutes

## Ingredients:

- 1/2 c. peanut butter
- 3/4 c. crispy rice cereal
- 1/2 c. butterscotch
- 1 pkg. white chocolate chips
- 1 c. chocolate chips

## Directions:

1. Prepare a baking sheet with parchment paper. Add the chocolate chips into a bowl and heat in the microwave until smooth.
2. In a second bowl, combine the butterscotch chips and white chocolate chips and cook in the microwave to make smooth. Add the peanut butter and cereal into this one and pour into the baking dish.
3. Spoon the other chocolate in lines across the mixture in the pan. Run a knife in the other direction to get the tiger stripes.
4. Cover the dish and place in the fridge for 10 minutes before slicing.

# Eggnog Fudge

For those who are looking for a holiday theme in their fudge, this eggnog option is going to check all of the boxes. Get ready to bite into something delicious!

**Prep Time**: 15 minutes

**Servings**: 36

**Cook Time**: 60 minutes

## Ingredients:

- 1 pinch ground nutmeg
- 1 tsp. rum extract
- 1 jar marshmallow crème
- 8 oz. vanilla candy melts
- 1/2 c. butter
- 2/3 c. eggnog
- 21/2 c. white sugar
- 1 tsp. butter

## Directions:

1. Prepare a baking pan by adding foil to it and greasing with some butter.
2. Combine the butter, sugar, and eggnog into a pan and bring to a boil on the stove. Boil for 5 minutes, stirring the whole time.
3. Add the marshmallow cream and vanilla candy pieces and mix to be smooth. Stir in the rum before pouring into the baking pan.
4. Sprinkle the nutmeg on top and allow to cool down for 30 minutes. Score into 36 pieces and let set in the fridge for an hour before serving.

# Chocolate Cherry Fudge

Cherry and chocolate come together to make this delightful treat you are sure to enjoy again and again. Start it ahead of time so you are ready to go.

**Prep Time**: 10 minutes

**Servings**: 32

**Cook Time**: 2 hours

## Ingredients:

- 25 c. halved candied cherries
- 1/4 c. pecan halves
- 1 tsp. almond extract
- 1/2 c. candied cherries, chopped
- 1/2 c. chopped almonds
- 1 pkg. chocolate chips
- 1 can sweetened condensed milk

## Directions:

1. In a baking pan, line some foil in it. Combine the chocolate chips and condensed milk together and microwave on high until chocolate is melted and stir.
2. Stir in the almond extract, chopped cherries, and chopped almonds. Pour into the prepared pan and spread evenly. Add the pecan halves and cherry halve son top.
3. Cover and let firm in the fridge for 2 hours before serving.

# Germany Chocolate Fudge

German chocolate is a great dessert to help with your sweet tooth. When you make it into a fudge, it is even better!

**Prep Time**: 15 minutes

**Servings**: 24

**Cook Time**: 60 minutes

**Ingredients:**

- 2 c. pecans, chopped

- 1/4 tsp. salt
- 1 can evaporated milk
- 2 Tbsp. butter
- 4 ½ c. white sugar
- 1 jar marshmallow crème
- 12 squares German sweet chocolate
- 2 c. semisweet chocolate chips

**Directions:**

1. Combine the marshmallow crème, German sweet chocolate, and chocolate chips together.
2. Combine the salt, evaporated milk, butter and sugar in a skillet and bring to a boil. Cook for 6 minutes and then pour this over your chocolate chip mixture. Stir in the chocolate mixture and pecans.
3. Spread into a prepared pan and give it time to firm up before serving.

# Mint Chocolate Fudge

Mint and chocolate come together in this delicious option that you will want to make again and again. It is simple to create and works any time of year.

**Prep Time**: 15 minutes

**Servings**: 32

**Cook Time**: 2 hours

## Ingredients:

- 1 drop green food coloring
- 1 Tbsp. peppermint extract
- 1 c. white confectioners' coating
- 2 tsp. vanilla
- 1 can condensed milk, sweet
- 2 c. chocolate chips

## Directions:

1. Prepare a baking pan with some waxed paper. In a pan, melt the vanilla with a cup of the condensed milk and the chocolate chips.
2. Spread half of this into the prepared pan and let it chill for 10 minutes. In a second pan, melt the white coating with the rest of the milk. Stir in the food coloring and peppermint extract. Spread this on the chilled chocolate layer until firm.
3. Spread the reserved chocolate over the mint layer and let it get firm.

# Pumpkin Fudge

This fudge is one of the best ones you can choose for those cool fall evenings. Whether you are heading to the pumpkin patch or just want something tasty to enjoy, take these out and see how delicious they can be!

**Prep Time**: 5 minutes

**Servings**: 21

**Cook Time**: 60 minutes

## Ingredients:

- 1 tsp. vanilla
- 2 Tbsp. butter
- 7 oz. marshmallow crème
- 1 c. white chocolate chips
- 1 tsp. ground cinnamon
- 3/4 c. canned pumpkin
- 21/2 c. white sugar
- 2/3 c. evaporated milk

## Directions:

1. Prepare a pan with some foil and butter the foil. In a pan, heat the sugar and milk. Bring this to a boil, stirring the whole time. Mix in the cinnamon and pumpkin and bring back to a boil.

2. Cook for another 18 minutes before taking off the heat and cooling for 3 minutes. Pour the white chocolate chips into a bowl and pour the fudge over it. Allow the chips to soften and stir to make smooth.

3. Pour in the rest of the ingredients and stir. Pour into a prepared pan. Allow time to cool down and then cut into squares to serve.

# Candy Cane Fudge

This is a great fudge to bring out if. You are preparing for the holidays. It is simple to make and has all the good tastes you need.

**Prep Time**: 5 minutes

**Servings**: 20

**Cook Time**: 2 hours

**Ingredients:**

- 1 dash green or red food coloring
- 1 1/2 c. crushed candy canes
- 1/2 tsp. peppermint extract
- 1 can sweetened condensed milk
- 2 pkgs. Vanilla baking chips

**Directions:**

1. Prepare a baking pan with some foil. Combine the milk and vanilla chips in a pan and let them heat up. Stir often until melted and then remove from heat.
2. When the chips are completely melted, stir in the candy canes, food coloring, and peppermint extract.
3. Spread out in the pan and chill for 2 hours before slicing and serving.

# Graham Cracker Fudge

With only three ingredients necessary, you will be able to make this fudge as often as you would like. It is simple and tasty any day of the week!

**Prep Time**: 15 minutes

**Servings**: 32

**Cook Time**: 2 hours

## Ingredients:

- 1 pkg. graham crackers, crushed
- 2 cans sweetened condensed milk
- 1 bag milk chocolate chips

## Directions:

1. Combine the condensed milk and chocolate chips in a pan and heat. Cook and stir to have the mixture melted and smooth. Stir in the graham crackers.
2. Pour this into a baking dish and smooth it out. Allow to cool down for 2 hours before serving.

# Mocha Fudge

For those coffee lovers, this is one of the best options to go with. A taste of coffee will make a big difference in giving you the best dessert!

**Prep Time**: 15 minutes

**Servings**: 16

**Cook Time**: 60 minutes

**Ingredients:**

- 1/2 c. pecan halves
- 1 c. chocolate chips
- 1/2 c. pecans, chopped
- 1 tsp. vanilla
- 3 Tbsp. butter
- 2 Tbsp. light corn syrup
- 1 c. milk
- 1 pinch salt
- 3 c. white sugar
- 1 Tbsp. instant coffee granules

**Directions:**

1. In a pan, stir the instant coffee, salt, and sugar. Stir in the butter, corn syrup, and milk. Heat up a bit to make sticky and solid.
2. Take off the heat and stir in the vanilla. When it is cool, beat with a wooden spoon to make the gloss go away. Add the chocolate chips and nuts and pour into a prepared baking dish.
3. Arrange the pecan halves on top and then allow to cool before serving.

# Cashew and Sweet Potato Fudge

Sweet potato may not be the first ingredient you think about with fudge, but it can be a tasty treat that you will want to make again and again. It is even a little healthier than other options.

**Prep Time**: 5 minutes

**Servings**: 32

**Cook Time**: 2 hours

**Ingredients:**

- 1/4 c. salted cashews
- 1/4 c. smooth cashew butter
- 1/4 tsp. nutmeg
- 1 tsp. salt
- 1 tsp. vanilla
- 1 Tbsp. warmed heavy cream
- 1/2 c. sweet potatoes, mashed
- 12 oz. white chocolate chips

**Directions:**

1. Prepare a glass dish with some baking spray and set to the side. Warm a glass bowl and add the white chocolate chips. Heat in the microwave until melted.
2. Stir in the nutmeg, salt, vanilla, cream, and sweet potatoes. Mix before adding the cashew butter to make smooth. Pour into a prepared dish.
3. Sprinkle on the chopped cashews and let it set for 2 hours before serving.

# Almond Joy Fudge

If you are a fan of Almond Joys, then you will want to make this fudge a bunch of times. It is better than the candy bar and will give you something delicious for any party.

**Prep Time**: 15 minutes

**Servings**: 20

**Cook Time**: 60 minutes

## Ingredients:

- 1/2 c. sweetened coconut flakes
- 1/2 c. almonds, chopped
- 1/4 c. butter
- 1 can sweetened condensed milk
- 3 c. chocolate morsels

## Directions:

1. Combine the butter, condensed milk, and milk chocolate in a double boiler over simmering water. Stir often and let the chocolate melt for 5 minutes.
2. Take off the heat and add the coconut and almonds inside. Pour into a baking dish and let it firm up in the fridge for one hour before serving.

# Chocolate Chip Cookie Fudge

Nothing is better than some cookie dough and this fudge is going to provide you with a healthy and great option any time you are hungry!

**Prep Time**: 15 minutes

**Servings**: 32

**Cook Time**: 60 minutes

**Ingredients:**

- 1 tsp. vanilla
- 1 c. mini chocolate chips, melted
- 1 pkg. confectioners' sugar
- 1 pkg. soft cream cheese
- 1/4 c. mini chocolate chips
- 3/4 c. flour
- 1 pinch salt
- 2/3 c. brown sugar
- 1/3 c. melted margarine

**Directions:**

1. Prepare a baking dish with some foil then set to the side. Add the brown sugar, salt, and melted margarine in a bowl. Stir in flour and knead it with the chocolate chips.
2. Form this dough into a disk and add it on a sheet of plastic wrap. Form into a square using your hands. place in refrigerator for 10 minutes before slicing into squares. Add to the fridge until later.
3. Mix together the confectioners' sugar and cream cheese in a bowl to make smooth. Stir in vanilla and

melted chocolate chips. Fold in the cookie dough pieces then spread out onto a prepared dish.

4. Leave in the fridge for an hour to make firm and then slice to eat.

# White Chocolate Caramel Fudge

Caramel and white chocolate will soon become some of your favorites when you decide to make this delectable fudge for all of your needs!

**Prep Time**: 15 minutes

**Servings**: 32

**Cook Time**: 60 minutes

## Ingredients:

- 1/2 c. caramel sauce
- 1 c. pecans, chopped
- 1/2 tsp. vanilla
- 4 Tbsp. butter
- 14 oz. sweetened condensed milk
- 3 c. white chocolate chips

## Directions:

1. Combine the butter, chocolate chips, vanilla, and milk in a bowl and heat up until melted. Stir to make smooth. Add the pecans and extract before scooping into a parchment lined tray and spread out.
2. Drizzle on the caramel sauce then swirl into fudge with a spatula. Chill until ready to serve.

# Rocky Road Fudge

If you are a fan of Rocky Road ice cream, then this is the fudge you want to try out as well. It is even better than the ice cream and you will find yourself reaching for more all the time.

**Prep Time**: 15 minutes

**Servings**: 20

**Cook Time**: 60 minutes

## Ingredients:

- 1 c. peanuts, salted
- 2 c. mini marshmallows
- 1 tsp. vanilla
- 1/4 c. butter
- 14 oz. sweetened condensed milk
- 2 c. chocolate chips

## Directions:

1. Combine the butter, chocolate, and milk in a bowl. Heat up until it is melted. Then add in the vanilla, peanuts, and marshmallows.
2. Scoop this onto a parchment lined tray and spread out. Chill until ready to serve and slice up.

# Nutella Caramel Pretzel Fudge

Nutella and caramel and everything mixes together to make a delicious fudge that everyone will want the recipe too.

**Prep Time**: 10 minutes

**Servings**: 20

**Cook Time**: 2 hours

**Ingredients:**

- 1 c. chopped pretzels

- 1 Tbsp. heavy cream
- 1 c. caramel bits
- 1 c. Nutella
- 10 oz. chocolate chips
- 1 tsp. vanilla
- 3 Tbsp. butter
- 1 can sweetened condensed milk

**Directions:**

1. Prepare a baking pan and line with some parchment paper. In a glass bowl, make a double boiler. Add the butter and condensed milk inside. When melted, add in the vanilla, chocolate chips, and Nutella.
2. Mix to combine and then pour into a prepared pan. In a bowl, combine the cream and caramel. Heat up until melted well.
3. Pour this over the fudge and swirl it around. Sprinkle the pretzels over it all and let it set 2 hours before serving.

# Cranberry Macadamia Nut Fudge

Any of these flavors on their own can be a treat. But when you combine them together, you have one of the best fudge recipes on our list.

**Prep Time**: 15 minutes

**Servings**: 32

**Cook Time**: 60 minutes

## Ingredients:

- 3/4 c. dried cranberries, reserve 1 Tbsp.
- 3/4 c. chopped macadamia nuts, reserve 3 Tbsp.
- 1/2 tsp. vanilla
- 4 Tbsp. butter
- 14 oz. sweetened condensed milk
- 3 c. white chocolate chips

## Directions:

1. Combine the milk, butter, and chocolate chips in a bowl. Heat up in the microwave until melted and smooth.
2. Add the nuts, cranberries, and vanilla inside. Scoop out into a prepared pan and spread out. Sprinkle the reserved cranberries and nuts on top and then let firm up before eating.

# Walnut Vanilla Fudge

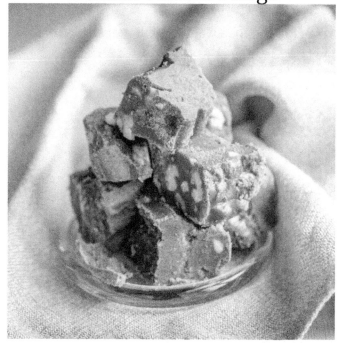

This is some of the best fudge that you can make. With just a few ingredients, it is creamy and rich for all of your needs.

**Prep Time**: 15 minutes

**Servings**: 21

**Cook Time**: 60 minutes

## Ingredients:

- 3/4 c. chopped walnuts with 2 Tbsp. reserved
- 1 tsp. vanilla
- 2 Tbsp. butter
- 7 oz. sweetened condensed milk
- 12 oz. white chocolate chips

## Directions:

1. Combine the butter, milk, and chocolate in a bowl and heat until smooth. Add the walnuts and the vanilla before spooning onto a prepared pan.
2. Spread the fudge out and then sprinkle on the reserved walnuts. Chill until ready to serve.

# Cranberry Cashew Fudge

Cranberries and cashew come together to make this tasty treat. It is everything you never knew. You needed some fudge.

**Prep Time**: 15 minutes

**Servings**: 32

**Cook Time**: 2 hours

## Ingredients:

- 1 tsp. vanilla
- 1/2 c. dried cranberries
- 1 c. salted cashews
- 1 c. chocolate chips
- 2 c. milk chocolate chips
- 1/2 tsp. salt
- 1/4 c. butter
- 1 can evaporated milk
- 1 ½ c. white sugar
- 1 jar marshmallow creme

## Directions:

1. Prepare a pan with foil. Then combine the butter, salt, evaporated milk, sugar, and marshmallow crème in a pan and bring to a boil until smooth.
2. After 5 minutes, take off the heat and add both chocolate chips until melted. Fold in the cranberries and cashews along with the vanilla.
3. Pour this into the prepared pan and then let firm for two hours before serving.

# Cinnamon Graham Vanilla Fudge

Cinnamon and graham crackers come together to make this the dessert that you need. It can work well in the summer when you are ready to go out camping.

**Prep Time**: 5 minutes

**Servings**: 32

**Cook Time**: 60 minutes

## Ingredients:

- 1 ½ c. broken cinnamon graham crackers
- 1/4 tsp. salt
- 1 tsp. vanilla
- 2 Tbsp. butter
- 2 c. white baking chips
- 1 pkg. cinnamon bun frosting

## Directions:

1. Prepare a baking pan with some foil and grease it up. Combine the bun frosting with the butter and white baking chips. Cook in the microwave until smooth.
2. Add in the vanilla, salt, and graham crackers. When smooth, spread into the prepared baking pan.
3. Chill and firm for an hour before serving.

# Brazilian Peanut Fudge

This one is a bit different than some of the others on the list, but can still cause a stir when you bring them to the next event!

**Prep Time**: 15 minutes

**Servings**: 32

**Cook Time**: 20 minutes

**Ingredients:**

- 1 can sweetened condensed milk
- 2 Tbsp. white sugar
- 1 pkg. tea biscuits
- 1 jar roasted peanuts

**Directions:**

1. Prepare a dish with some waxed paper. Pulse the biscuits and peanuts together to make a course flour. Add the sugar to mix too.
2. Pour the milk into this and make a dough. Move to the prepared dish and push it down into an even layer. Allow to set a minimum of 15 minutes before storing.

# Strawberry Fudge

For our final recipe, let's add in a bit of strawberry to the mix. This will help give you all the great flavors that you want and need in a lovely bit of fudge!

**Prep Time**: 15 minutes

**Servings**: 32

**Cook Time**: 2 hours

## Ingredients:

- 2 egg whites, beaten
- 1 c. strawberry preserves
- 1/4 tsp. cream of tartar
- 1/2 c. water
- 2 c. white sugar

## Directions:

1. Prepare a square pan and then take out a saucepan. Combine the cream of tartar, water, and sugar and bring to a boil. Cook util it forms into a syrup and then add the strawberry preserves. Return to a boil.
2. Take off the heat and add this in with the beaten egg whites. Beat until thick and fluffy. Pour into a pan and cool for 2 hours until firm.

# Conclusion

Many people avoid making fudge because they think it is too difficult to make. But as you can see with some of the delicious recipes in this guidebook, it is possible to make some of the best fudge, without all the hassle. Whether you want to stay with some of the simple chocolate recipes or you are looking to make something brand new, you will want to take a bunch of bites out of this fudge and make it all your own. Dive right into some of these amazing recipes and see how great they can be today!

Printed in Great Britain
by Amazon